CENGAGE Learning

Poetry for Students, Volume 3

Staff

Series Editors: Marie Rose Napierkowski and Mary Ruby.

Contributing Editors: Amy Francis, Carol Gaffke, David Galens, Lynn Koch, Marie Lazzari, Mary Onorato, James Person, Jr., Susan Salas, Anna J. Sheets, Diane Telgen, Lawrence J. Trudeau.

Managing Editor: Drew Kalasky.

Research: Victoria B. Cariappa, *Research Team Manager*. Andy Malonis, *Research Specialist*. Julia C. Daniel, Tamara C. Nott, Tracie A. Richardson, and Cheryl L. Warnock, *Research Associates*. Jeffrey Daniels, *Research Assistant*.

Permissions: Susan M. Trosky, *Permissions Manager*. Kimberly F. Smilay, *Permissions Specialist*. Steve Cusack, *Permissions Assistant*.

Production: Mary Beth Trimper, *Production*

Director. Evi Seoud, *Assistant Production Manager*. Shanna Heilveil, *Production Assistant*.

Graphic Services: Randy Bassett, *Image Database Supervisor*. Robert Duncan and Michael Logusz, *Imaging Specialists*. Pamela A. Reed, *Photography Coordinator*. Gary Leach, *Macintosh Artist*.

Product Design: Cynthia Baldwin, *Product Design Manager*. Cover Design: Michelle DiMercurio, *Art Director*.

Page Design: Pamela A. E. Galbreath, *Senior Art Director*.

Copyright Notice

Copyright © 1998
Gale Research
835 Penobscot Building
645 Griswold St.
Detroit, MI 48226-4094

This book is printed on acid-free paper that meets the minimum requirements of American National Standard for Information Sciences—Permanence Paper for Printed Library Materials, ANSI Z39.48-1984.

ISBN 0-7876-2724-0
ISSN 1094-7019

Printed in the United States of America.
10 9 8 7 6 5 4 3

On the Pulse of Morning

Maya Angelou 1993

Introduction

Poet, playwright, composer, actress, singer, and human rights activist, Maya Angelou is heralded as a "people's poet," her work written in a common voice which is both accessible and emotionally charged. In 1993, when Bill Clinton decided to invite a poet to read at his first presidential inauguration ceremony—for the first time since Robert Frost stood on stage with John F. Kennedy in 1961—he chose fellow Arkansas native Angelou to write a poem celebrating the new beginning of his presidency. The panoramic piece that Angelou composed, "On the Pulse of Morning," reached millions of television viewers. Its popularity proved so great that it was published as a cassette and chapbook in 1993. The work was distributed to schools, libraries, cultural centers, and book stores nationwide.

Appropriate for what Clinton promised would be a new era in American history, "On the Pulse of Morning" is an optimistic piece that offers hope for the future by embracing positive aspects of the past. Angelou builds the poem on a simple foundation, "A Rock, A River, A Tree," from which point she searches the distant past to provide answers for the present as well as advice for America's future. Drawing different races, cultures, and religions together, the poem invites all of humankind to return to the foundations that made the country great, including basic values and an appreciation of nature. Angelou calls upon ancient voices in hopes that "Each new hour holds new chances / for a new beginning."

Author Biography

Born on April 4, 1928 in St. Louis, Missouri, Maya Angelou spent most of her childhood in the rural, segregated environment of Stamps, Arkansas, raised by her maternal grandmother after the divorce of her parents. She emerged from a disturbing and oppressive childhood to become a prominent figure in contemporary American literature, and Angelou's quest for self-identity and emotional fulfillment is recounted in several volumes of autobiography, beginning with *I Know Why the Caged Bird Sings*, which chronicles the author's life up to age sixteen. As a black girl growing up in a world whose boundaries were set by whites, Angelou learned pride and self-confidence from her grandmother, but the author's self-image was shattered when she was raped at the age of eight by her mother's boyfriend. Angelou was so devastated by the attack that she refused to speak for approximately five years. She finally emerged from her self-imposed silence with the help of a schoolteacher who introduced her to the world's great literature. The author spent much of her troubled youth fleeing various family problems. She was homeless for a time, worked on and off as a prostitute, and held a variety of jobs in several places as a young adult, changing her name to Maya Angelou when she became a cabaret dancer in her early twenties. Eventually she became an actress, joining the European touring cast of *Porgy and Bess*, but concern for the welfare of her young son, born when Angelou was just sixteen, eventually brought her back to the United States.

By the time she was thirty, Angelou had made a commitment to becoming a writer. Inspired by her friendship with the distinguished social activist author John Killens, she moved to Brooklyn to be near him and to learn her craft. Through weekly meetings of the Harlem Writers' Guild she learned to treat her writing seriously. At the same time, Angelou made a commitment to promote black civil rights. The next four volumes of her autobiography —*Gather Together in My Name* (1974), *Singin' and Swingin' and Gettin' Merry Like Christmas* (1976), *The Heart of a Woman* (1981), and *All God's Children Need Traveling Shoes* (1986)—trace the author's psychological, spiritual, and political odyssey. Angelou recounts experiences such as encounters with Malcolm X and Dr. Martin Luther King, Jr., her personal involvement with the civil rights and feminist movements in the United States and in Africa, her developing relationship with her son, and her knowledge of the hardships associated with the lower class of American society. In *All God's Children Need Traveling Shoes*, Angelou describes her four-year stay in Ghana where she worked as a free-lance writer and editor.

Angelou's poetry, which is collected in such volumes as *Just Give Me a Cool Drink of Water 'fore I Diiie* (1971) and *And Still I Rise* (1976), has also contributed to her reputation and is especially popular among young people. It is particularly noted for its use of short lyrics and jazzy rhythms.

Angelou recently directed national attention to humanitarian concerns with her poem "On the Pulse of Morning," which she recited at the 1993 inauguration of President Bill Clinton.

Lines: 1-8

In these opening lines, Angelou sets the scene and tone of the poem. She places three objects before the reader: "A Rock, A River, A Tree," but doesn't give a specific location. These three elemental pieces seem removed from any landscape, and, from the capitalization of each name, it has been speculated that Angelou intends each to stand for itself in a type of grandeur. The poem goes on to explain that these objects are "hosts to species long since departed," still surviving though their "tenants" are long extinct, further implying they carry a certain "historical wisdom." From here the poet lists a few of those creatures known only from their "dried tokens" dug up and reassembled in museums. Their "sojourn," or temporary stay here, ended in a "hastening doom," which they had no way of predicting or preventing. "Any broad alarm" of their extinction is now dwarfed by the mountain of history between their time and the present.

If lines 7 and 8 are read aloud, it's possible to hear the rich sounds Angelou crafts into the poem. The repetition of long vowel sounds and the internal rhyme of "Doom / is lost in the gloom" perhaps reflect the somber mood Angelou is setting while describing these extinct creatures.

Lines: 9-13

Line 9 marks a shift in time, a move from looking back at history to the present. The "Rock" from the first stanza now has a voice, which it is using to cry out "clearly, forcefully." It offers the reader an invitation to climb up and get a better perspective of where America might be heading in a journey toward a "distant destiny." But like a teacher the Rock warns against seeking any shelter or hiding place behind it in the darkness. "Shadows" have long been the places that cause fear, where bad things lurk under beds or behind closet doors. They are also, literally, the absence of light: within shadows it is difficult to see clearly. For the religious, light is divine; for philosophers it is knowledge. Believing this, divinity and knowledge are absorbed by the stone but absent in its shadow.

Lines: 14-18

In the third stanza, the Rock continues its lesson, addressing the reader directly as "You, created only a little lower than / the angels." Here the poet seems to close the gap between man and heaven, the stone again raising the reader. This Rock has seen dinosaur come and go, and now humans, who, it notices, "have crouched too long in *the bruising darkness* … face down in ignorance." Angelou's verb choice "bruising" in line 16 may describe how a shadow casts a blue-black mark across a face, reminding the reader of conflict and its dark wounds. The speaker suggests humans have been hiding, not looking up toward the light, afraid of what they might learn.

Lines: 19-23

Angelou ties the third and fourth stanzas together with the line "Your mouth spilling words *Armed for slaughter." She may have broken the line here to force the reader to pause in the white space between, to guess "what kind of words?" before finishing the sentence. The harsh words "spilling" from humans' mouths seem to be pouring out of our control, "armed for slaughter," ready for a fight with anyone listening. But the Rock warns again, summarizing "stand upon me;* But do not hide your face." People may wear many "faces"—student, laborer, wife, father—that are different, but they all provide an identity and a sense of individuality.

Lines: 24-26

With the beginning of a new section, Angelou introduces a new speaker, the "River," which, in a song, invites the reader to come closer and "rest here by [her] side." To get to the River, the reader had to cross "the wall of the world," which may be some real geographic feature, or just representative of a boundary or obstacle on humankind's journey.

Lines: 27-34

The River compares each person in America to

"a bordered country / … perpetually under siege," relating the troubles of an entire nation back to its million voices. The River explains what the country has done wrong: gone to war for money, polluted waters with machines and factories, ignored the needy. Angelou describes the toxic waters as a "current of debris upon [the River's] breast," giving nature gender and perhaps reminding that it is "Mother Nature" who is being destroyed. There is a place for Americans to rest on her shore, but only if they "study war no more."

Lines: 35-40

If people come "clad in peace," the River offers them a song: a gift the Creator gave before the tallest tree ever broke soil as a single shoot. "I and the / Tree and the Rock were one" once, the River explains, in a time before recorded history, in a time before man began drawing boundaries and daring others to cross these lines.

"Cynicism" is the belief that people are motivated by selfishness, and the "bloody sear" across their brows may be a reminder of the mark Cain was cursed to wear for his selfish act—the murder of his brother. "When you yet knew you still knew nothing" perhaps means a humbler or even wiser time; Plato said "True wisdom is knowing we know nothing."

Lines: 41-49

Using a list—or a litany—to create a wide panoramic scene of diverse peoples, Angelou introduces the reader to a new speaker, the Tree. It seems everyone is here to listen, regardless of culture, occupation, which gender with which they fall in love, or to which God they pray. This diverse list works to welcome any and all to the foot of the Tree, much like the engraved invitation at the base of the Statue of Liberty, "Bring me your tired, your poor, your huddled masses."

Lines: 50-54

In this short stanza the poet repeats again the invitation to "plant yourself beside the River," the entire mass of humankind welcome to hear the song. The Tree has many symbolic meanings, not the least of which is the concept of extended family —or "Family Tree." A tree also has roots that stretch into the very earth. In these symbols Angelou is reminding the reader of their place both within their family (blood relations and other) and within nature.

Lines: 55-63

Calling Americans "descendants of passed-/ On traveler" the River asks the reader to consider both their own past and the past of the country as a whole. There is a reminder that all Americans are immigrants, that they are "just passing through." Angelou follows this up by directly addressing the Native Americans, those who lived in this country centuries before Europeans ever arrived: the Pawnee tribe, Apache, Seneca; the people who first named the rivers and trees and mountains. These people who once rested with the River were "forced on bloody feet" by the visitors in their land to work and mine.

Lines: 64-69

In these lines Angelou advances the poem through another list of diverse people, the rhythm of the names keeping beat, Arabs and Eskimos sharing company in the same breath. She begins the list with people who came to this country to escape religious persecution or find a better life for their family, and concludes with those who were forcibly uprooted and "bought *Sold, stolen, arriving on a nightmare* Praying for a dream." This "dream" may be a reference, or allusion (a reference within a literary work to another work), to Martin Luther King's famous "I Have a Dream" sermon, which became an anthem for the Civil Rights Movement of the 1960s.

Lines: 70-79

In the second section of the poem, the stanzas become longer, building in imagery and force. In lines 70-74 the poet returns to the comforting refrain "root yourselves beside me." The three voices—Rock, River, Tree—may be a single "I," the whole of nature speaking. Back in lines 55-56 Angelou writes "each of you … … *has been paid* *for," and a similar statement is made in line 74: "your passages have been paid." Who's paid for these passages? What have America's ancestors done to insure the journey? Regardless of origin, the Rock*Tree/River *asks humankind to "lift up [our] faces … For this bright morning dawning for you." These lines mirror the second stanza, where Angelou offers images of shadow and light. This is also the first indication to the poem's title, perhaps working to create an overall theme or mood of dawning hope. Yet Angelou also cautions that the hardship that has led to this new day should never be forgotten: "wrenching pain,* Cannot be unlived." She warns that America must learn from its dark past so that when new problems arise they can be overcome; "if faced / With courage, [history] need not be lived again."

Lines: 80-83

Following this revelatory stanza, where the three voices merge in a call to a bright new morning, this shorter stanza closes the entire second section on a quiet, consoling note. The lines become short—most less than four words—the poet perhaps wishing to slow the pace before the complete stop of the section break. For the third time Angelou invokes the refrain "lift up your eyes." The dream the slaves prayed for might be alive again if a new generation "will study war no more" and instead "give birth again" to a peaceful world.

Lines: 84-92

Beginning the third section with a single addressing line, Angelou maintains the encouraging, powerful tone of the Rock/River/Tree, yet the speaker is not specifically identified. She asks America to "Sculpt [your private need] into *The image of your most public self." This is an elusive line in its generalization, perhaps telling instead of showing, but if it is broken down into its parts, a central tension reveals itself. The line asks the reader to sculpt or transform their most private needs into something that can be shared with others, the personal made public. Angelou doesn't develop further what "private needs" may be, but most critics have speculated a reference to the most basic human freedoms. In this sense these lines are a call to action, an encouragement to emphasize the importance of human rights. Whereas before Americans are asked to lift up their eyes, line 87 asks the same of their hearts, the center of all life and emotion. There are "chances* For a new beginning" if people can divorce themselves from fear and unchain themselves from their violent ways. "Yoked" refers to the wooden harness which keeps an ox secured to the plow it drags, a heavy bar across the animal's shoulders and fastened with straps around its body.

Media Adaptations

- The 1993 inaugural ceremony at which Angelou first read the poem is documented by James Earl Jones in the video *An American Reunion: Inauguration 1993*, available from Timelink on VHS.

- A recording of Angelou reading "On the Pulse of Morning" during the inauguration is also available on audio cassette from Random House (1993).

- A selection of poems read by the author, *Still I Rise*, includes the title poem, a piece she wrote for the Negro College Fund. It is also by Random House (1996).

Lines: 93-101

The sections are shorter and more frequent as Angelou nears the end of the poem. In the fourth section she returns to the locale of the second stanza, perched on the back of the land looking out toward the future. "The horizon leans forward," providing room for "new steps." This metaphor of taking steps may mean literally to walk forward as well as take "steps" or actions to ensure that past mistakes are not repeated. The speaker now reveals itself as the voice of America, the "Country" and all the trees, rivers, rocks, people, and animals of which it is composed. "Midas" in line 100 refers to the fabled king who could turn any substance to gold with his touch, including, he regretfully discovered, those he loved, leaving him with a castle filled with lifeless riches. A mendicant is a beggar; like the privileged standing next to the homeless before the Tree in line 47, all are equal in the larger "pulse of this fine day."

Lines: 102-110

In this closing section the title of the poem reveals its meaning, the theme of a new dawn for humankind coupled with the pulse that courses through America's common veins. The lists of various peoples earlier in the poem now become the simple image of family: when people look up and out at their future, they are looking at their "sister's eyes" and their "brother's face." Whereas most of the poem asks the reader to rest and listen to the wise teacher, these last lines implore speech. A "simple" lesson, Angelou refrains certain lines as many as four times throughout the poem, the tone taking on an almost lulling, song-like effect. The first step to this new day is a simple but meaningful action. Look up and out and say "Good Morning."

Knowledge and Ignorance

Written in the personae of nature as teacher, "On the Pulse of Morning" offers a clear message of how America should prepare for the future. Beginning as early as the second stanza, the Rock offers an invitation to stand upon its back to face a distant destiny. This heightened perspective offers a clear vision of what is on the horizon, a theme that recurs throughout the poem in lines such as "lift your faces," "lift up your eyes," "look up and out and upon me" and "look up and out *And into your sister's eyes." The metaphor of lifting one's eyes to the light is deeply rooted in religious and philosophical literature. One of the most famous pieces is Greek philosopher Plato's theory that describes man as a being living in a cave, isolated and trapped in his ignorance. The only knowledge that reaches him is the coin of light from a distant entrance, hardly enough to illuminate any writings on the cave walls. For man to become truly "enlightened," Plato suggests, he must move toward the light and out into the brighter world of knowledge. Angelou suggests a similar metaphor when the Rock warns "But seek no haven in my shadow,* I will give you no hiding place down there." In some cases "ignorance is bliss," a haven where it's easier to ignore actions than take the responsibility and burden that comes with knowledge. And the speaker makes the ignorance clear: America's near past plays host to such atrocities as racism, genocide, world war, slavery, environmental destruction, and prejudice. Americans have "crouched too long in *the bruising darkness* … Facedown in ignorance." The key to "a bright new morning," Angelou proclaims, is to step out of our dark past and lift our faces, hearts and eyes toward the light.

Pride

A common theme in many of Angelou's poems, prose, plays, and television documentaries is the value of pride even in the most desperate of situations. A sense of pride is what sustains people even when they are enslaved, harassed, humiliated, and degraded. Rather than show personal defeat in the face of oppression, Angelou states, people should lift their faces and walk proud, for someday they will be rewarded for their hardships. Angelou's ancestors (as well as many other Americans') were those who were "sold, stolen, arriving on a nightmare *Praying for a dream." Growing up in a segregated, racist South where whole white communities once gathered outside elementary schools to scream racial slurs at black children, Angelou learned the value of personal strength in seemingly hopeless times. "History, despite its wrenching pain," Angelou suggests, "Cannot be unlived, but if faced* With courage, need not be lived again." This courage and pride may carry people through difficult times, but they must also "free ourselves from mental slavery" as well. As the poem comes to a close, the speaker warns "Do not be wedded forever *To fear, yoked eternally* To brutishness." By standing proud in the face of history's wrenching pain and freeing oneself from the bonds of anger and ignorance, Americans can "look up and out" toward "the pulse of this new day."

Violence and Cruelty

When Angelou accepted the offer to commemorate the inauguration of Bill Clinton into the presidency, she was faced with a monumental task: write a poem that offers the American people hope while being honest about this country's violent and cruel history. Perhaps deflecting some of this burden by creating a personae speaker to convey the positive and negative messages, Angelou balances the two by using the violent past to offer a lesson for the future. Some say humans are an inherently violent creature, "mouths spilling words *Armed for slaughter*" *from the very beginning. "Each of you" the River accuses, "[is] a bordered country,* Delicate and strangely made proud, *Yet thrusting perpetually under siege." Is America made proud by its "armed struggles for profit," claiming glorious victory after the Gulf War? The picture the poem begins with is fairly grim: America's forefathers forcing the native people from their land and families to wander on bloody feet; kidnapping cramped boatloads of Africans from across the ocean to become sub-human slaves; even today the environment is embattled, the oceans and rivers clogged with "collars of waste" and "currents of debris." The image of a person "yoked eternally* To brutishness" calls to mind an animal enslaved by a heavy harness of cruelty. These are the bonds and "wrenching history" the speaker reminds the reader of so that they may overcome the past. Emphasizing that personal cruelty—prejudice—is the most damaging, Angelou gathers a diverse crowd to stand before the tree of wisdom, Jew next to Arab, homosexual next to Catholic priest, brother and sister, all equal in the pulse they share: "No less to Midas than the mendicant, / No less to you now than the mastodon then."

Topics for Further Study

- Write a poem using "the voice of nature." Drawing from nature, address the American people with a lesson on how to survive in the coming millennium. Give examples from the past to illuminate what we might do to better humankind and survive what some see as an impending doom.

- Some critics have accused President Clinton of insincerely "piggy-backing" on Angelou's diverse cultural views by choosing her to read at his inauguration (he chose her instead of the appointed Poet Laureate of the United States). Others aim their protest at Angelou herself, questioning the value of a poem commissioned for a politician's gain. Do you think the unique circumstances surrounding this poem's creation and publication in any way affect its "authenticity" or "value?" How so?

- Make a list of various peoples living in your neighborhood based on culture, race, and religion. How many different groups are represented? Compare your list with classmates and explore why it may or may not be different from your own. How diverse or segregated is your neighborhood?

Style

"On the Pulse of Morning" is written in free verse, which means its form grows from the changing moods and urgency of its subject matter rather than from a set pattern of "traditional" poetic rules. Angelou has divided the poem into five sections, each constructed of stanzas of varying length. Few lines extend beyond ten words, which perhaps asks the reader to slow down, pausing often to digest the images before beginning the next line. Whereas long lines tend to build momentum like a train going down hill, shorter lines break up a poet's images into smaller, digestible chunks. Although the rhythm and sound of these shorter lines are slower, they don't feel choppy or stilted.

The word "stanza," directly translated from Italian, means "room," so it's useful to think of each stanza as a place the poet collects her images, a place to explore and move through. Angelou varies her stanza length greatly in the poem, from one to ten lines, depending on the subject matter she needs to contain. The shorter the stanza, the more emphasis each line has to carry, framed by so much white space. These stanzas, grouped into distinct sections, give a larger framework to the long poem. Treating the panoramic poem perhaps like a musical piece composed from several movements, Angelou weaves these individual sections into a fluid whole. This technique lends itself to recitation; the poem gains power as it is read aloud, the rhythms and sounds conveying meaning as much as the words themselves.

Historical Context

One of the distinct features of "On the Pulse of Morning" is the extent to which it is firmly rooted in its historical context. Angelou's reading during Clinton's 1993 inauguration reached a worldwide television audience, followed shortly after by the poem's individual paperback, cassette, and videotape publication. For many months "On the Pulse of Morning" seemed to be everywhere— shopping–mall bookstores, high–school classrooms, coffee tables—even in grocery–store checkout lines. The poem became inextricably bound with Clinton's ascendancy, with a "new" era in American politics. Clinton was the first Democrat elected to the presidency in twelve years. Many saw his term in office as a chance for a fresh beginning, an opportunity to undo the snarled mess that American politics had become; these feelings and values were personified in the imagery of Angelou's poem.

The early–1990s proved to be the beginning of the budget cutting that would whittle the National Endowment for the Arts (NEA) down to a fraction of its potency. Many Republicans, responding to pressure from the Christian Coalition, argued to abolish the agency, citing its valueless "funding of pornography" (a charge that stemmed largely from a collection of photographs by Robert Mapplethorpe featuring nude men). The NEA underwrites the work of emerging artists and writers so they may pursue their craft and teach others. When Republicans learned that some of these artists were producing work that dealt with social issues in a raw and graphic manner, they attacked the endowment for funding indecency and "anti-family" values. Clinton, a Democrat, platformed his campaign on the value of education and the diverse arts, pledging to protect the NEA's budget if he were elected. For some, his invitation to Angelou seemed exemplary of his dedication to the arts; to others, it was an associative political maneuver that stood hollow of sentiment.

"On the Pulse of Morning," with its diverse celebratory tone and hopeful message, was written as an address to a nation living the last decade of the twentieth century. Any time an artist is invited to create an "occasion" piece, the theme of the day drives the poem's course. Angelou knew this as she wrote the poem, and perhaps responded to current news of wars and racism in-between its lines. The world was in a violent and changing time, coalition forces having recently liberated Kuwait during the Gulf War. On television American planes were still shooting down the stray Iraqi jets that crossed into the "no fly zone." Israeli helicopter gunships assassinated Hisballa leaders in Southern Lebanon. An April 29th acquittal of Los Angeles, California, policemen involved in the Rodney King beating triggered the worst race-driven violence and looting in U.S. urban history, killing fifty and injuring some 2,000 others. In Germany neo-Nazi skinheads attacked gypsies and Turkish working–class families.

In 1992 America's population topped 250 million. The national debt exceeded 3 trillion dollars. The country seemed to be "thrusting perpetually under siege," itself only months removed from an international war to protect the world's oil supply. Angelou had a huge task at hand. Warning against another "armed struggle for profit," she addressed the nation with the hope that the country would "study war no more," choosing instead to lift their collective faces, hearts, and eyes toward the first pulse of light breaking over the horizon.

Critical Overview

Because "On the Pulse of Morning" is a poem written specifically to celebrate Bill Clinton's 1993 inauguration, it entered the public's awareness having virtually bypassed the normal gauntlet of criticism that follows most poetry publications.

Broadcast on international television shortly before chapbook copies were distributed to bookstores, not many critics have come forward to offer specific commentary. Moreover, by debuting the poem in front of an audience of millions—who embraced the poem's artistry—Angelou preempted the critics' opportunity to influence potential readers before they had a chance to hear or read the work. After millions had praised the poem, many critics reasoned that it might seem petty to criticize such optimism in the face of such vast public approval.

Perhaps Angelou's reputation preceded her, guaranteeing the poem's validity: she is the author of over thirteen novels, autobiographies, and poetry collections. For many she is considered one of the most powerful voices of contemporary literature. Some critics point to her varied careers in the arts to emphasize her driving spirit. Lynn Bloom in *Dictionary of Literary Biography* noted that Angelou "is forever impelled by the restlessness for change and new realms to conquer." This hunger for change is common in much of Angelou's work, along with, as Gloria Hull stated in *Belles Lettres*, the theme of "human oneness in diversity, the strength of blacks in the face of racism and adversity."

What Do I Read Next?

- Angelou's complete body of poems is assembled in *The Complete Collected Poems of Maya Angelou*, a 273–page softcover published in 1994.

- Another poet who is renowned for her use of everyday speech and colloquial voices is Gwendelen Brooks. Her collected poems, entitled simply *Blacks* (1994), is available from Third World Press.

- When it came time for his second term inaugural ceremony in 1997,

Clinton invited relatively unknown Arkansas poet Miller Williams to compose a verse. His poem, the similarly themed *Of History and Hope*, is included in the poet's most recent collection, *The Ways We Touch* (1997).

- Much can be learned about Angelou's poetry by reading about her diverse life. The first of her five autobiographies—and best-known prose work—is *I Know Why the Caged Bird Sings* (1970), a moving account of her troubled childhood.

Sources

Bloom, Lynn, *Dictionary of Literary Biography*, Volume 38: *Afro-American Writers after 1955*, Gale, 1985.

Hull, Gloria, "Maya Angelou" in *Belles Letters*, Spring, 1991, pp. 2-4.

For Further Study

Cudjoe, Selwyn, "Maya Angelou and the Autobiographical Statement" in *Black Women Writers (1950-1980)*, edited by Mari Evans, Garden City, NY: Anchor Books, 1984.

> Focusing primarily on Angelou's five autobiographies, this essay provides insight on her passion for individual identity, a theme the poem also reflects.

Hagen, Lynn, *Heart of A Woman, Mind of a Writer, and Soul of a Poet: A Critical Analysis of the Writing of Maya Angelou*, University of America Press, 1997.

> One of the several books of comprehensive Angelou criticism to appear as a result of her renewed prominence following the inauguration, this critical text explores the poet's use of colloquial urban language as a source for her musical poetry and prose.

Neubauer, Carol E, "Maya Angelou: Self and a Song of Freedom in the Southern Tradition" in *Southern Women Writers: The New Generation*, edited by Tonett Bond Inge, University of Alabama Press, 1990, pp. 114-42.

> In this essay Neubauer uses close

readings of Angelou's poetry to illustrate the connection between individual images of Black hardship and the larger picture of an oppressed race surviving in America during the poet's lifetime.

Lightning Source UK Ltd.
Milton Keynes UK
UKHW020651190722
406066UK00009B/1090